# Inspire

## THE ART OF
## LIVING WITH
## NATURE

# Inspire

## THE ART OF LIVING WITH NATURE

50 BEAUTIFUL PROJECTS TO BRING THE OUTSIDE IN

*Willow Crossley*

CICO BOOKS
LONDON NEW YORK
www.rylandpeters.com

Published in 2014 by CICO Books
an imprint of Ryland Peters & Small
519 Broadway, 5th Floor, New York NY 10012
20–21 Jockey's Fields, London WC1R 4BW

www.rylandpeters.com

10 9 8 7 6 5 4 3 2 1

A CIP catalog record for this book is available from the
Library of Congress and the British Library.

ISBN: 978 1 78249 095 1

Printed in China

Project editor: Gillian Haslam
Copy editor: Helen Ridge
Design: Laura Woussen
Photography: Emma Mitchell

To my amazing, most wonderful
mother, Kate. You have taught me
everything I know and helped me
every step of the way for as long
as I can remember. With all my
love, I dedicate this book to you.
x x x

# Contents

# Introduction

I am neither a florist nor an interior designer. I am just flower mad with a serious passion for decorating.

I grew up in deepest rural Wales but, if I am completely honest, my love of nature wasn't full blown then. Although my childhood was rooted in the countryside, from an early age my outdoor life was firmly connected to homemaking. I picked wildflowers to decorate my bedroom or pressed them to become pictures. Walks were spent nose down, treasure-hunting for my museum of relics, and when I made a den with my brothers, I insisted on being chief decorator.

I can vividly remember being given a bunch of lilies on my fourteenth birthday by my friend Alex, which was quite an unusual present for a teenage girl at the time. We were both at boarding school and didn't own a vase, so the lilies had to live in a basin. But I absolutely loved them and loitered in the bathroom, admiring their beauty. They made me feel inexplicably happy and marked the start of my love affair with flowers. I've never looked back, and have been without food (sometimes) to finance my habit.

When I was about fifteen, I became bored by my sleepy country horizons and longed for something glitzier and fast paced. I eventually moved to London, where life was intoxicating. I made new friends, went to university, got a job, and loved it all. But, ten years later, I began to want the calmer, prettier way of life again. This coincided perfectly with Chaz, my (now) husband, moving to a remote vineyard in the South of France, and I followed him.

We spent the next five years in rustic bliss. When not crushing grapes, I was filling trugs with lavender, trawling the local brocantes or markets for fabrics and treasures, and beachcombing. I would bring home my spoils, excited by how they turned our house into a home. I started creating still-lives and vignettes with them as a way of saving space, but finally ran out of room. It was then that I started collecting and buying with other peoples' homes in mind. There began my interior styling and dressing business.

It's unthinkable for me not to have flowers at home, but should there be a surface without a vase on it, I'll put shells, fir cones, crystals, herbs, or plants there instead. Picking is easy in late spring and summer, when the hedgerows are bursting with growth, but it does become harder in the winter to rely on treasures from the countryside or garden.

In this book I want to show how natural elements—and I don't just mean flowers—bring an affordable and accessible dimension to an interior. For natural, think the opposite of manmade: anything that has lived, evolved, or grown. I've divided the book into five chapters—Woodland, Flora, Fauna, Beach, and Edibles—and show how my favorite elements from these groups can be used to create an impact in many different settings. There are ideas for living rooms, bedrooms, and bathrooms; table settings for feasts and al fresco picnics; and show-stopping flower arrangements. Put simply, I hope you'll share my view that bringing nature into your life also brings in the magic.

CHAPTER
ONE

Woodland

It's midsummer as I write, and I can barely move for Queen Anne's lace, or cow parsley *(Anthriscus sylvestris)*. This small, umbrella-shaped wildflower emerges in late spring from the hedgerows like clouds of cream lace and continues flowering for months. For me, it is like the swallows: a sign of early summer and a reminder of my country childhood.

# Cow Parsley

A huge bunch of Queen Anne's lace will look ravishing on its own in a vase, but it is just as beautiful paired with lilac, as shown here, which flowers at the same time. Late-flowering white narcissi, tulips, and alliums also make beautiful companions. Meanwhile, old glass vases filled with shorter individual stems highlight their frothy, relaxed nature to perfection.

The fact that I can pick armfuls of Queen Anne's lace on my doorstep, sear them momentarily, and they will last for weeks puts it up there in my top-ten favorite flower list.

If you dip the stems into boiling water, then plunge them into cold water up to their necks for 10 minutes, Queen Anne's lace can last for a surprisingly long time.

## INGREDIENTS
Large pitcher or jug

Queen Anne's lace (cow parsley)

Lilac (*Syringa*)

Garden clippers (secateurs)

At the risk of sounding like a lunatic, acorns always make me think of fairies. When I was small, I had a book about fairies living in acorns, which I've never forgotten. After all these years, acorns still have a magic association for me, and I love any excuse to turn them into house decorations.

# Acorn Napkin Decorations

Here, I've used acorn cups, saved from my endless foraging, and combined them with acorns that I've made using paper balls and crocheted beads. These fit snugly into the cups, and their gold-leaf coating makes them even more magical than one of nature's acorns.

These little treasures need to be used where they're going to be noticed without merging into the background. I love slotting them into napkin rings and tying them onto gift tags. They would also make divine corsages for an autumnal wedding.

You can also display these acorns piled high in glass jars, or fill the base of a hurricane glass vase with the acorns and place a large church candle in the middle, perfect for inside and out. Alternatively, for something a little glitzier, after you've painted the balls in the gold paint, sprinkle them with an even dusting of very fine glitter for mini disco acorns!

If you want to make these decorations at a time of year when acorns aren't scattered on the ground under the trees, you can cheat and buy little bags of them online.

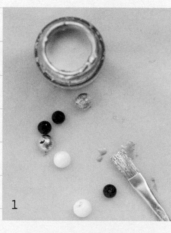

1

2

## INGREDIENTS

Newspaper or protective sheet

Paper balls

Crochet beads

Gold-leaf paint

Flat-edged paintbrush (optional)

Glue gun and white glue

Acorn cups on their stems

Raffia

Linen napkin

Luggage label (optional)

1 Lay down the newspaper or protective sheet. Gently drop the paper balls and crochet beads into the gold-leaf paint, making sure that the paint covers them completely. You may want to use a paintbrush to push them around in the paint and/or give them a bit more coverage once you've fished them out. Let them dry completely.

2 Use the glue gun to put a tiny blob of glue in the bottom of each acorn cup and drop in a ball or bead. Let the glue dry.

3 Tie some raffia around a folded napkin and slot an acorn sprig behind it.

4 If you wish, add a luggage label with the guest's name to the stalk.

# Apples and Blossom

**Blossom can be a bit of a tricky character. It's so ravishing but the second you bring it indoors, it tries to throw its petals all over the floor. You'd never choose blossom for its longevity, but it's definitely right for a short-lived show-stopping display, when you want to create something big, blowsy, and dramatic, to grab people's attention. It also shouts "spring" in a way that will make you smile.**

Blossom is the word given to flowers from fruit trees. Cherry, apple, and plum are the most common here in the UK, and they appear in a heavenly array of pinks and white. Quince is a real favorite, with its delicious pale coral, cupped blooms that remind me of old-fashioned roses. I always settle on one particular blossom as my favorite until I find another beauty, then I'm swayed all over again.

I've used a mix of apple and cherry blossoms here, both from my garden. Keeping things simple, I displayed them by themselves, but for variation and a bit of excitement, I slotted the glass vase of blossom inside a slightly larger one, which I lined with sliced apples.

The apples will look good for a few hours, making this a wonderful decoration for a party. Once they are too brown for your liking, simply lift the vase of blossom out and enjoy it on its own, apple-free.

If you are going to bring blossom indoors, pick it when it's not quite in bloom and keep it as cool as possible. It should last longer that way.

The insides of apples go brown pretty quickly when they're exposed to the air. To prevent this, soak them in lemon juice for a while before arranging them.

## INGREDIENTS

10 apples

Sharp knife

Bowl, for soaking the apples

1 lemon

5 long blossom stems

Garden clippers (secateurs)

2 tall glass vases, one that will sit inside the other, leaving a 1-in (2-cm) gap between them

1 Cut the apples in half. Try to cut diagonally through the core so you are left with a pretty star shape in the middle.

2 Put all the apples in a bowl of cold water and squeeze the juice of the lemon into the water. Let the apples soak for 10 minutes.

3 Meanwhile, arrange the blossom in the small vase and fill it with water. Place the vase in situ.

4 Put the vase containing the blossom inside the larger vase.

5 Cut the apples into 1-in (2.5-cm) slices, then slot them, one by one, into the gap between the two vases.

# Disco Branches

**Using branches as decoration is one of my favorite, most cost-effective tips, especially for parties, where creating the same impact with flowers would be seriously expensive because you would need so many.**

## INGREDIENTS
Branches with leaves
Tissue-paper tassels
Very large glass jar

When Chaz and I got married, the inside of our wedding marquee looked like an enchanted forest. We created two "trees" from leafy oak branches and erected them down the middle of the tent and had the most wonderful arrangements on each table that resembled mini oak trees.

My "disco tree" here was made using a branch from one of the trees in the garden that needed pruning—but by no means am I suggesting you start lopping down trees left, right, and center! I then hung colorful paper tassels from tiny barbs on the branches. I have to admit that I didn't make these tassels myself, but you could try making your own if you have the time.

Branches covered in leaves —it really doesn't matter from which tree—are obviously preferable for this project, but you can still do wonderful things with branches when they're bare. For a festive party, try wrapping bare branches in different-colored yarn threads and hanging Christmas baubles from them. They'll be slightly more time-consuming to make, but you'll be able to keep them forever and they would look great all year round, too.

If you add water to the jar,
the branches should last
happily for days.

The Victorians were crazy about ferns. So much so that there was an entire movement, known as pteridomania, or fern fever, which swept through Britain between 1837 and 1914. Beautiful and undemanding, ferns flourish in most environments, and growing them became a passion that anyone could enjoy.

# Floating Ferns

## BRANCHING OUT

Using wreaths of different diameters looks much more effective than sticking to just one size. To display, simply space them out along a bare branch with fishing wire, fixed to the wall or ceiling.

Their hardiness makes ferns perfect for these hanging wreaths. They don't last an eternity, but you will get about three days out of them. There are thousands of different types of fern, but I'm afraid I'm not knowledgeable enough to suggest specific varieties. All I would recommend is to use pliable fronds with plenty of evenly spaced leaves. The wreaths are easier to make in spring when the fronds are young—there's nothing more annoying than one snapping just before you finish a wreath.

If you're finding the ferns
hard to bend, take a sharp knife
and score the whole way down the
back of their stem.

1

2

## INGREDIENTS

4 fern fronds (the longer, the better)

Green floristry stub wire

Garden clippers (secateurs)

Metal circular wreath

Fishing wire

Tree branch

1 Starting at the stalk end of one frond, wrap stub wire over and around the base of each leaf and around the metal circle. Wrap the wire around tightly, keeping it as close to the circle as possible so there are no gaps. Stop winding just before you reach the tip of the frond.

2 Start again with a new frond, making sure you tuck the beginning of it under the tip of the frond you've just wired.

3 Keep going until you've covered the whole circle in ferns. Cut off any protruding pieces of wire.

4 Attach a length of fishing wire to the top of the wreath and hang where it can be admired.

# Dried Flower Treasures

## INGREDIENTS
Bunches of dried Queen
Anne's lace (cow
parsley)

Brown sticky tape

**I am incapable of going for a walk in the country and coming back empty-handed. Like a magpie, I always find something irresistible to pick up.**

In winter, when there's much less to pilfer—the leaves are gone and the birds are firmly holding on to their feathers—the most worthwhile treasures are dried flowers hiding out in the hedgerows. Queen Anne's lace (cow parsley) is my absolute favorite. In fact, we can no longer get inside our little potting shed after my rather excessive picking, and Chaz has banned me from bringing any more home.

The potting shed is now my dried flower gallery—anything remotely pretty and dried gets stuck to the wall with plain brown tape. I just love these silhouettes dancing across the white background and the haphazard, chaotic look of it all.

If you don't have a wall that you can decorate, think about framing the flowers instead. I find bigger flowers have greater impact and are less fussy than lots of little ones. Architectural, spiky flowers like Queen Anne's lace also look very effective coated in thick white paint.

I love to go for a walk in the local countryside and return home with a perfect, uneaten fir *(Abies)* cone or, better still, a larch *(Larix)* branch laden with mini cones. They feel so wintry and I always associate them with cozy, Christmassy suppers.

# Festive Fir Cones

Here, I've simply painted their tips in quite muted neutrals and blues, left over from decorating the house, and turned them into name card holders for a festive supper. But I also love the idea of going for a slightly wackier, neon theme. Another option would be to use glue in the place of paint, followed by a dusting of ultra-fine glitter.

## INGREDIENTS

Fir cones

Leftover paint in muted neutral shades and blues

Paintbrush

Glue (optional)

Very fine glitter (optional)

Name cards

## WIRED-UP CONES

Fir cones are very amenable to work with and can be wired easily. Push a length of florists' wire through the cone segments, then twist the ends of the wire over each other until they are as tightly wound together as possible. The cones are now ready to be slotted and secured into any arrangement, a Christmas wreath, or even tied to other fruits and flowers. Alternatively, hang them from branches.

**I adore Christmas, especially because it gives me a legitimate reason to decorate the house from top to bottom with an extravagant amount of festive treasures.**

# The Holly and The Ivy

## INGREDIENTS

Long branches of holly, preferably with berries

Long stems of ivy

Adhesive putty (Blu-Tack), optional

Add drama to a winter table by trailing lengths of greenery down the middle of it, then dotting candles or tea lights in between the spaces.

Christmas trees still delight me, and each year I am transported back to that feeling of childish excitement that began on December 1st, when we opened the first door on our Advent calendar. At school, the homemade baubles and festoons with which we decorated our classrooms were hideously and competitively glittering. But, back then, I found them beautiful, especially as we children had all saved pocket money for weeks to create the maximum amount of magic.

Twenty years on, I still believe that less is definitely not more, and at Christmas I like to go all out, in a natural, green, non-shiny way. My mother deserves the credit for this, and I confess that I've copied what she does at home. It's very, very simple. All you need are long trails of ivy and tall branches of holly, with berries if possible. The aim is to decorate as many surfaces as possible with holly and ivy: tuck it behind paintings and above doorframes; weave it around photos and lamp bases on side tables. If you have shelves similar to these, either rest the holly and ivy along the shelves or, if they won't stay put, use a little bit of adhesive putty to hold them down.

CHAPTER
TWO

*Flora*

**I didn't really "get" hellebores until I moved to the country, where the garden is bursting with them. They always seemed rather rarified, seldom appearing in the local florists, as if they were too superior to hang out with boring carnations (*Dianthus*).**

# Experimental Hellebores

Since moving home, though, I've come to know the real reason they keep such a low profile—it's simply down to the fact that once they've been picked, they demand some looking after to prevent them from drooping after a couple of hours. One important thing I've learned is that they need to be picked early in the morning (see the project steps overleaf for additional tips). Also, in my experience, white hellebores seem to last longer when picked than their darker siblings.

Hellebores have now become one of my favorite flowers, and I'm so excited when they start to poke through the earth in January. As lucky as I am to have them growing in my garden, I'm a still bit stingy about picking huge bunches of them. And when I see them for sale at £5 a stem, having an armful of my own makes me feel guiltily extravagant. I much prefer to pick one or two real beauties at a time and mix them with lots of greenery for a big arrangement. They look heavenly with euphorbia, pussy willow (*Salix discolor*), evergreen *Viburnum tinus*, unfurling beech (*Fagus*) leaves, and sprays of blossom.

If you can't get your hands on any greenery or if you prefer to display the flowers on their own, creating a "scientific" display, as I've done here, requires very few flowers but still looks really striking. I've been collecting old green glass medicine bottles and Pyrex beakers and flasks used in school science experiments for quite a while now and I love the contrast of their functional lines with the ornamental ruffles of the hellebores.

Although the white *Helleborus niger* is known as the Christmas rose, hellebores are not members of the rose family.

## INGREDIENTS

Purple hellebores

Sharp garden clippers
(secateurs)

Boiling water

Old Pyrex science
beakers and flasks

Old green glass
medicine bottles

1 Cut the stems on the
diagonal with clippers
(secateurs), so they will
take up more water.

2 Plunge the ends
immediately into 2½in
(6cm) of boiling water for
about ten seconds, to
prolong their life, but
make sure that the steam
doesn't touch the petals.

3 Put the hellebores into
the containers filled with
cold water, removing any
leaves that will be under
water.

4 Keep the displays in as
cool a room as possible and
change the water every
couple of days.

**I've put the two flowering bulbs narcissi and hyacinths under the one heading because, for me, wherever one goes, the other has to go, too. I've also planted them in exactly the same way.**

# Spring Flower Wine Boxes

Narcissi and hyacinths remind me of Christmas at home when I was younger. My mother would secretly plant up the bulbs in September and then, just before the holidays, she would bring out crates of ravishing narcissi and hyacinths, magically about to flower, from the cold boot room. They made the house smell heavenly for weeks on end. Perhaps even more special were the hyacinths that opened obligingly in mid-January, cheering us, and the house, up once the Christmas decorations had come down.

As a child, my summer vacation was always spent on Tresco, a tiny island in the Isles of Scilly, off the coast of Cornwall. Before tourism took over, the main industry was growing and exporting the most exquisitely scented narcissi I've ever come across (happily, this practice is continuing on the neighboring island of St. Mary's). I still associate the two—the summer vacation and the narcissi—with each other, which might explain why I love them both so much.

I adore narcissi and hyacinths as cut flowers, too, but they last so much longer when potted as bulbs. And when the flowers are past their best, you can plant them in your garden to bloom again the following year.

It's important to use "prepared" hyacinth bulbs and "indoor" Paperwhite or Soleil d'Or narcissus bulbs for these winter-flowering displays, as outdoor garden bulb varieties won't flower in time for Christmas.

## INGREDIENTS

Grit, stones, or pebbles

Wine box

Bulb fiber, such as peat or coir

Paperwhite narcissus "indoor" bulbs or "prepared" hyacinth bulbs

Stems of pussy willow (*Salix discolor*)

Trowel

Sphagnum moss

1 Sprinkle a generous layer of grit over the bottom of the wine box, to help with drainage.

2 Dampen the bulb fiber and add a thick layer on top of the grit, up to about 3in (8cm) from the top of the box.

3 Place the bulbs on top, making sure they're not too closely packed together (although there's nothing worse than a sparsely filled container) and add the accompanying stems of pussy willow in and around the bulbs.

4 Using the trowel, fill in around and just over the bulbs with more fiber and decorate the top with sphagnum moss.

5 Give the bulbs a drink of water and hide them away in a cool, dark place (ideally, at around 48°F/9°C).

6 Check on the bulbs now and again while they are in hiding. They won't need regular watering, but if the fiber is no longer damp, trickle on a little water. Be careful not to saturate the fiber because this will make the bulbs go moldy.

7 The first shoots of the Paperwhites should be emerging after 6–10 weeks, and after 8–10 weeks for the hyacinths. Bring the box into the light to force the shoots into flower. This should take about 3 weeks.

**For me, a red amaryllis at Christmas is as festive as the wreath on the door, which puts it up there with holly and mistletoe, maybe even the tree itself. There's something majestic about its upright bearing and velvety petals—it is definitely a high-ranking member of the flower kingdom.**

# Majestic Amaryllis

You often see amaryllis potted in containers or baskets or as extravagant cut flowers in vases, but I prefer to grow them in old pickle jars, as shown here. I think this gives them a botanical chic, rather like turning them into a museum specimen for you to watch growing taller and taller until they flower.

Amaryllis always seem to fall over under their own weight, but these jars act as a support from every angle, which makes them practical as well as beautiful. Curiously, amaryllis don't really need soil—just a tiny trickle of water every so often will do, to keep the roots wet.

## INGREDIENTS

Newspaper or protective sheet

Potted amaryllis bulb, with its green shoot just visible

Old glass pickle jar, at least 12in (30cm) tall

1 Lay out the newspaper or protective sheet. Transfer the bulb from its pot by holding the stem close to the bulb and pulling very gently. Be aware that the potting compost will go everywhere!

2 Shake and dust off as much potting compost as you can and place the bulb at the bottom of the jar.

3 Trickle in enough water so that the roots are wet. Sit back and watch the magic. Once the flower bud has appeared, it will shoot up very quickly.

One of my earliest floral memories is making daisy-chain bracelets for my brothers. They never really got the point of them but I still love making them, and I just adore these simple, cheery blooms that grow almost everywhere in the world.

# Daisy Wreath

My creation here is basically a bigger, grown-up version of a daisy chain. It's just as easy to make, although it might take a tiny bit longer. You need more than just daisies, though, because their foliage isn't bulky enough to give a dense background, and their stems aren't always strong enough to poke into the florists' foam. Sprigs of buckthorn (*Rhamnus*) and rosemary, with their good, strong stems, provide this. If you don't have buckthorn, silvery Eleagnus leaves will work just as well. Failing that, just make sure you use foliage with firm stems.

## INGREDIENTS

Wreath of florists' foam, about 12in (30cm) in diameter

Sprigs of buckthorn (*Rhamnus*)

Sprigs of rosemary

Garden clippers (secateurs)

Strong, green string

Scissors

Armful of *Anthemis punctata* subsp *cupaniana* daisies

1 Soak the florists' foam according to the manufacturer's instructions (mine needed 5 minutes) then let it drain for another few minutes so it's not too saturated and dripping everywhere.

2 Cut the buckthorn and rosemary sprigs at an angle so they can be fed easily into the foam.

3 Cut a length, about 20in (50cm), of green string and tie it around the top of the wreath to make a hanging loop.

4 Working on a flat surface, lay out the foliage and fill the wreath on the front and sides with sprigs of greenery.

5 When you have an even cover of foliage, start filling in with the daisies. For a natural look, vary their lengths, although shorter stems are easier to poke into the foam, especially when cut at an angle. Snip off or tuck in any wayward trailing bits once the wreath is hanging.

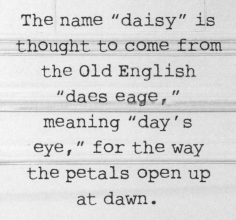

The name "daisy" is thought to come from the Old English "daes eage," meaning "day's eye," for the way the petals open up at dawn.

# Dazzle with Anemones

**Anemones are ridiculously pretty, so wispy and fragile with their paint-box silk petals and frilly leaves. They come in all shades of pink, blue, crimson, purple, scarlet, and white. There are three varieties that flower in spring, summer, and fall, so you can find them for most of the year. They are also amenable in arrangements and deceptively strong—you just need to be careful not to bash them about because their petals can tear or become stained by specks of pollen.**

## INGREDIENTS

White anemones with purple centers

Dark purple ranunculus

White ranunculus

*Alchemilla mollis*

Solomon's seal (*Polygonatum* x *hybridum*)

Sharp garden clippers (secateurs)

Small containers, such as narrow-necked glass jars

Larger ceramic pots in muted colors

Here, I've mixed white anemones with purple centers with dark purple and cream ranunculus, to keep the colors quite restrained, and then added my favorite fillers of *Alchemilla mollis* for greenness and Solomon's seal (*Polygonatum* x *hybridum*) for a contrasting leaf shape.

Anemones are quite an extravagance to buy, but one way to eke them out while still creating a dazzling display is to line them up in individual containers. Try using traditional milk bottles, mini jam jars, test tubes, or vintage shot glasses.

1 Cut the stems of all the flowers on the diagonal.

2 Fill the containers with water.

3 Arrange groups of all the flowers in the large ceramic pots and reserve one or two blooms for the small glass jars.

Anemones will last about 6-8 days in a vase, and you can help them along by removing any leaves below the water line. They are very thirsty flowers, so check their water levels frequently.

# Wayward Tulips

**Tulips are definitely one of my favorite flowers. They remind me of feeling like a grown-up for the first time. After leaving school, I moved to London and suddenly realized I could do exactly what I wanted. There was no one to make decisions for me, and no one to hurry me along while I spent an hour weighing up the pros and cons of buying flowers over food. Invariably, the flowers won and I would spend the week eating just baked potatoes. But I had a heavenly tulip backdrop and couldn't have been happier.**

When I was a student, tulips were always my "go-to" flowers—better than a carnation and less obvious than a rose. They were available almost everywhere and, for the most part, just about affordable. The large supermarkets sometimes sold them for less than a carton of milk, which would send me into a frenzy of excitement and I would skip home happily with bunches of them wrapped in cellophane.

Tulips haven't always been quite so ubiquitous. In seventeenth-century Holland, at the peak of their fame, tulips were so highly prized that a single bulb would sell for ten times the annual income of a skilled craftsman. They became a measure of status, and the more tulips you owned, the wealthier and more powerful you were thought to be. The tulip market crashed as quickly as it evolved, and many economists today consider "Tulipmania" to be the first ever speculative bubble.

I'm no longer a student but still feel that a ready-made bunch of flowers is an extravagance, and as much as I love an exquisite "floristy" bouquet, I've never been able to justify buying one for myself. Instead, I will buy a bunch of one variety and then mix it with masses of foliage at home.

I know not everyone lives in the countryside and/or has gardens or generous neighbors who are happy to give you some of their foliage, but creating swanky arrangements really doesn't have to cost a fortune. The only part of this display that I paid for is the tulips. The rest I pilfered from local hedgerows, trees, and gardens, with permission, obviously! I used branches of budding beech (*Fagus*) trees, Solomon's seal (*Polygonatum* x *hybridum*), blossoming hawthorn (*Crataegus*), *Viburnum tinus*, and red and yellow bicolored parrot tulips.

Arranging with tulips is pretty simple; they have strong, long stems and look wonderful with everything. However, take into account that they keep growing once they've been picked and often lean in a particular direction or droop down as they try to get closer to the light. I personally love this wild, out-of-control look, but if you prefer something neater, perhaps you should rethink using tulips. They will look ravishing to begin with, but after a day or two, when they have opened up, the display can appear a bit wayward. When I made this arrangement, the tulips were closed and the blossom was in bud. As the days went by and everything began to bloom and open, all the elements worked around each other in the magical way that nature always seems to contrive.

Picked tulips generally don't live for very long—on average only 5–7 days—but you can help them live longer. Cut their stems diagonally under running water. The diagonal cut increases the surface area so the stem can take up more water, while making the cut under water stops air getting into the stem. Every two days, cut 1in (2.5cm) off the bottom of the stems, to sustain the water intake. Put a few copper coins in the vase—for some reason, this helps to keep the stems upright. Tulips are very thirsty flowers so keep them topped up with clean water.

### INGREDIENTS

Branches of budding beech (Fagus) trees

Blossoming hawthorn (Crataegus)

Vintage white porcelain pitcher

Viburnum tinus

Red and yellow bicolored parrot tulips

Solomon's seal (Polygonatum x hybridum) in muted colors

1 Arrange the branches of beech and hawthorn in the pitcher first, to create a base shape.

2 Add the viburnum, tulips, and Solomon's seal.

3 Stand back from the pitcher to see if the display can be improved and move the plants accordingly.

## DECLARATION OF LOVE

The language of flowers was popular in the Victorian era, and tulips were generally seen as a symbol of love. If you were given a red tulip as a declaration of love, you could either accept the romantic gesture by taking the tulip with your right hand or decline it with your left.

As well as their obvious beauty, the hydrangeas' generous size makes them doubly useful and lets you create something bold with just a few giant blooms. Here (and for the ball on page 72) I've used dried hydrangea heads, but fresh blooms would work just as well.

3

## INGREDIENTS

Green ribbon or string

Copper beech (Fagus sylvatica atropunicea) leaves

Oak (Quercus) leaves

Strong florists' wire

Hydrangea stems

Rhododendron stems

Sprigs of rosemary, preferably in flower

Garden clippers (secateurs)

Scissors

1 Measure how long you want the garland to be with some ribbon or string. Add an extra 8in (20cm) on each end to use as hanging loops. Lay out the foliage along the ribbon like a long, fat sausage.

2 Hold the florists' wire tightly and, starting at one end of the "sausage," carefully wrap it up and around the foliage and ribbon to bind them together. Secure the wire at the other end.

3 Feed in the hydrangea, rhododendron, and rosemary along the garland wherever you want them. Depending on where the garland is to be displayed, it may be easier to hang up the foliage "sausage" first and then add the flowers along its length. In this way, less of the garland will come adrift when you carry it into position.

There are no hard-and-fast rules for making this project, but I find it's best to start by laying out the foliage like a long, fat sausage-the fatter, the better.

# Hydrangea Garland

Hydrangeas remind me of my wedding day. Chaz and I were married in September in the house in Wales where I grew up. Happily for me, the garden had a lot of hydrangea bushes. My mother—gardener extraordinaire—spent months pruning and nurturing so that everything would be at its peak for our big day. The hydrangeas were perfect, and we had spectacular banks of greeny-blue ones to decorate the church, tent, and tables.

# Primroses for Tea

**Primroses (*Primula vulgaris*) epitomize spring, and the first yellow sightings of them give me hope that winter has finally ended. They used to grow much more abundantly in the wild and became a rural industry in the nineteenth century, when trains transported posies of them in tissue-lined boxes to the cities.**

Now they grow more sparsely in hedgerows and woodland, and I would never pick them to make an arrangement. Instead, I buy or dig up an existing plant growing in my garden and then, when the arrangement is no longer looking its best, I plant it back in the ground, somewhere cool and shady, where it will thrive and multiply, knowing that I'll have twice as many to bring inside next year.

There's something ethereal about primroses and, to exaggerate their fragility, I chose the oldest, most delicate china for their containers. However, with china there's no in-built drainage, so you need to improvise and make your own. I sprinkle gravel or wood chips at the bottom before potting and usually the plants stay perky.

Primroses do like to be as cool as possible—they really can't cope with being hot and in direct sunlight, where they will wilt sulkily right in front of your eyes. This display lasted happily for weeks in my chilly bathroom. I've also decorated an Easter tea table with primroses in china. They look heavenly dotted around in cups on saucers mixed in with actual cups of tea and cakes.

### INGREDIENTS

Gravel or wood chips

Pretty china bowl and cup with saucer

2 primrose (*Primula vulgaris*) plants

Potting compost

Sphagnum moss

1 Put a ½-in (1-cm) layer of gravel or wood chips at the bottom of the bowl or cup.

2 Position the primrose plants in the center and fill in any gaps with potting compost.

3 Decorate the top of the potting compost with pieces of sphagnum moss, and water well.

In the Middle Ages, primroses were used to make love potions. It was also believed that primroses had great healing powers and could even cure paralysis.

# Dramatic Lilac

According to folklore, it's bad luck to bring lilac *(Syringa)* indoors. There is a morbid association, as the scented flowers were used to mask the smell of death when a body was laid out at home. Although I am quite superstitious—I won't walk under ladders or over three drains, or pass another person on the stairs—I'm afraid I love lilac too much to be deterred by such beliefs.

I was excited to discover three huge lilac bushes in our new garden, and even more so when they turned out to be white, pale lilac, and deep lilac. The flowers look heavenly displayed on their own, and if you keep them out of direct sunlight and remove all leaves below the water line, they can last for ten days. They appreciate an occasional misting, too.

For this project, however, I wanted to make quite a big, dramatic display, so decided to combine the lilacs with other country blooms. Keeping it tonal and seasonal, I added extra-long delphiniums, Solomon's seal *(Polygonatum x hybridum)*, bluebells *(Hyacinthoides non-scripta)*, and a mix of green and silvery leaves from the garden.

Some people think it's pointless, but I'm convinced that searing flowers does prolong their life. Different types of flower require different lengths of time but, as a general rule, anything floppy likes about 30 seconds in boiling water, followed by a long drink in deep, cold water. As the lilac had such woody stems, it needed the longest amount of time of all the flowers I used (see opposite), while the bluebells needed only 10 seconds.

The amount of stem you sear is in proportion to the length of stem cut. Flower guru extraordinaire Sarah Raven sears 10 per cent. So, if the stem is 20in (50cm), sear around 2in (5cm). Leaving the stems in for too long will cook and disintegrate them.

## INGREDIENTS

Pink lilac *(Syringa)*

Deep blue delphiniums

Solomon's seal *(Polygonatum x hybridum)*

Bluebells *(Hyacinthoides non-scripta)*

Mix of green and silvery leaves

# Ever-Obliging Forsythia

**Forsythia and I never used to get on. Yellow is my least favorite color, and I've always just ignored the shrub when it flowers in early spring. However, this year we had a truce and I let it hang out in the kitchen for a good few weeks. I have to say I loved it. It was incredibly obliging—far more amenable than blossom, which instantly drops its petals all over the floor—and lasted for ages.**

The handy thing about forsythia is that it's everywhere, from gardens and parks to schools and parking lots, and there's no escaping its beaming yellow spikes. It's also hardy and happy to be picked while the flowers are still lime-green and before the leaves have appeared, which means you can bring it inside and watch it blossom in front of you.

For this vivid arrangement, I've mixed forsythia with lime-green hawthorn *(Crataegus)* and frothy sycamore *(Acer pseudoplatanus)* blossom and leaves in a clashing red vintage fire bucket. Forsythia appears before many of the other spring-flowering shrubs. If you want to mix it with something else and don't want to splash out on store-bought flowers, think about creating an architectural, spiky display with some twigs and velvety pussy willow *(Salix discolor)* from the hedgerows instead.

## INGREDIENTS

Sycamore *(Acer pseudoplatanus)* blossom and leaves

Forsythia stems

Hawthorn *(Crataegus)* stems

Red vintage fire bucket

1 Cut all the stems on the diagonal, then plunge 10 per cent of the length of the stem into boiling water for 20 seconds (see note on page 64).

2 Fill the bucket with cold water and start adding the sycamore stems.

3 Add the forsythia and hawthorn, continually standing back to check you are happy with the shape you are making.

Peonies are one of the most requested flowers for weddings, where they are mostly mixed with other equally frothy, soft, pale flowers, such as lilac (*Syringa*), love-in-a-mist (*Nigella damascena*), roses, and hydrangeas. With that in mind, this project shows how wonderful they look when arranged informally in a chipped pot with much stronger, brighter, deeper colors. Despite their rather blowsy, fragile appearance, peonies are actually quite hardy, which makes them ideal for creating huge, dramatic displays.

The peony is the traditional floral emblem of China, the state flower of Indiana, and one of the symbols to mark a 12th wedding anniversary.

INGREDIENTS

Pale pink peonies

Pink Queen Anne's lace, or cow parsley (*Anthriscus sylvestris*)

Vivid pink carnations (*Dianthus*)

Deep pink sweet Williams (*Dianthus barbatus*)

Granny's bonnet (*Aquilegia vulgaris*)

*Tellima grandiflora*

Rosemary

*Alchemilla mollis*

Beech (*Fagus*) leaves

# Exquisite Peonies

I was never really sure what to do with a peony—they're so exquisite, so expensive, and so beautiful that I worried that however I chose to arrange them, I wouldn't do them justice. I used to put them in a vase on their own with no interfering friends or foliage, which meant they could be admired all alone with nothing else to detract attention. Now that I'm more aware of what's out there, and probably because I now have a garden of my own, I'm becoming braver and like to mix things up a bit.

# Scented Pelargoniums

**There's nothing secretly innovative going on here. I just wanted to show how incredibly beautiful lots and lots of pelargoniums (commonly known as geraniums) can look when they're grouped together *en masse*.**

This is the interior of my parents' greenhouse—a place they practically decamp to in early summer. The smell as you walk through the door is out of this world. A blast of pungent, heady, citrus scent takes my breath away and transports me instantly to the Mediterranean.

These plants are another genus that I'm slowly learning more about and appreciating for their forgiving nature. Unless they get seriously frosted in winter, they survive very happily on a windowsill, not even demanding water in cold months. They perk up miraculously each spring and respond energetically to being snipped back.

Every season new species of pelargonium come into my life and I'm left trying to work out my favorite all over again. This year, the two at the top of my list are 'Dark Secret' and 'Australian Mystery'. My overall winner, though, has to be 'Citronella' for her delicious citrus-scented leaves, which also happen to keep mosquitoes at bay.

### INGREDIENTS
Assorted scented pelargoniums

Terra-cotta pots

Potting compost

I have a real thing about pompoms and have always loved the idea of creating them out of flowers. They are quite time-consuming, though, so I haven't made as many as I'd like to yet.

# Hydrangea Pompom

1 Tie the fishing wire around the middle of the ball of florists' foam, leaving two long ends.

2 Secure the wire in place with thumbtacks (drawing pins). I used about eight, to be sure it would hold.

3 Knot the two ends of the wire together.

4 Break off small florets from the dried hydrangea heads, making sure that their stems are strong enough to pierce the foam ball.

5 Start inserting the florets into the ball, keeping them all very close together to hide the foam beneath. When this starts to get a bit fiddly, you will find that pushing them in with a pair of small scissors is much more effective than using clumsy fingers.

6 Continue until the whole ball is covered. Hang it from the knotted wire in a place where it can be admired and enjoyed.

## INGREDIENTS

Fishing wire or ribbon

12-in (30-cm) diameter ball of florists' foam

Thumbtacks (drawing pins)

4 dried hydrangea heads

Small scissors

*Gypsophila paniculata*, or baby's breath as it is more commonly known, is another great flower to use in these pompoms. You can use it fresh, and it will still look pretty when it has dried.

**The Cubs think that alliums are huge dandelion clocks. They stand side-by-side, huffing and puffing at them but can't understand why the tiny florets don't fly away.**

# Starry Alliums

I love these giant pompoms with their spherical heads of starry flowers. I prefer to leave them in the garden when they're flowering, but if I do ever have an impressive clump and feel a few won't be missed, I can't resist cutting them to create dramatic displays.

Here, I've used brightly colored empty olive oil cans from Greece, and mixed the alliums with irises and bolted leeks. Alliums and leeks are members of the onion family, and I have to admit this wasn't the sweetest-smelling arrangement. However, adding a drop of bleach to the water stopped the oniony smell and also extended the arrangement's life.

## INGREDIENTS

Colorful olive oil cans

Alliums

Bolted leeks

Irises

1 Remove the lid of the olive oil can, if necessary, and discard. Clean the inside of the can thoroughly with hot, soapy water. Rinse well.

2 Add the alliums, leeks, and irises, but don't overfill the can as a sparse arrangement looks more effective.

If the alliums have been
squished, revive and fluff up
their flattened heads by holding
the stem upside down between
your palms, then rolling it
back and forth.

## ETHEREAL DRIED ALLIUMS

When the flowers go over, pick them and hang them upside down to dry. You will end up with beautiful spiky balls that look wonderful sprayed with gold or silver paint.

Here they are hanging from the mantelpiece with cotton thread. As they are fairly fragile, you need to be as nimble-fingered as you can when playing around with them. Thread a needle with the same color thread as your background and slot/weave it through the stalk, tying a knot at the end.

**Clematis dances up the front of our house, looking beautiful for a few weeks every year and then vanishing, but I've never actually picked it to include in an arrangement before.**

# Clematis Wreath

Clematis grow on vines, which means they are basically a wreath waiting to happen. They are calling out to be tied into divine little circles and festooned on walls and doors. I love hanging a collection of them all together.

Clematis has a dark side. All parts of the plants are toxic, and should you eat them, you will experience a severe burning sensation and develop mouth ulcers.

### INGREDIENTS

Clematis vine with leaves and flowers

Sharp garden clippers (secateurs)

Natural-colored raffia

Scissors

**1** Cut the desired length of vine and tie the ends together discreetly with raffia.

**2** Tease the vine into a wreath shape.

**3** For something a little jazzier but also very pretty, tie tiny pieces of colorful ribbon or fabric here and there onto the wreath.

# *Auricula Theater*

**My auricula (*Primula auricula*) obsession comes from my mother, although a few years ago, I thought they were just fancy pansies—nothing particularly wonderful and definitely nothing to get excited about.**

But then I started to look at them closely, at their exquisite patterning, striking bold colors, and delicate frilled petals. I'm now a complete auricula addict. I could happily sit and stare at them for hours on end and can totally see why people once built "theaters" especially to display them.

Some people believe that auriculas came to England with the Huguenot weavers when they were forced to flee France in the sixteenth century. Today, over 2,000 varieties of the little beauties exist, with societies dedicated to the growing and cultivation of new species.

I've shown my auriculas, displayed singly in old terra-cotta pots for maximum impact, in my own version of a theater—a vintage wooden cupboard with a dark turquoise background. Ideally, auriculas like to be outside, but they don't mind being brought inside temporarily if needs must. They aren't too fussy about their living conditions. Just make sure not to splash their leaves when watering, and protect them from direct sunlight—they prefer to be kept somewhere shady.

## INGREDIENTS

Auricula (*Primula auricula*) plants

Old terra-cotta pots

Potting compost

Vintage cupboard

Traditional auricula theaters consisted of tiered shelves, with an overhanging roof to protect the plants from the direct sun and rain. The interiors were made of black velvet, which gave the petals a dramatic backdrop.

**Lavender reminds me of pre-Cub life in France, where Chaz and I lived in the south for years. By mid-May, without fail, the fields around our house were a dazzling deep purple.**

# Lavender Table Setting

## INGREDIENTS

Pretty blue ceramic and terra-cotta pots

Gravel, for drainage

Lavender plants

Potting compost

## DRYING LAVENDER

If you would like to dry lavender, the best time to do so is just as the flowers begin to open, when they have the strongest scent. Cut the stems as long as you can and let them dry in the shade for about four or five days. They will dry more effectively if well spread out so that air can circulate around them.

In this part of France, lavender grew everywhere you looked. I loved picking huge bunches of it for the bedrooms, and would spend hours making tiny lavender bags, sewing them from scraps of linen found on my trawls through the local *brocantes* and filling them with dried lavender heads.

For this table setting, I've simply put single lavender plants into pretty pots and kept the rest of the décor quite tonal (as well as the many shades of blue and purple, there are also pink and white varieties of lavender). I also love slotting a few strands of lavender into a rolled napkin and tying it with a length of raffia. It all brings back memories of long, relaxed lunches, which, as I write, seem a million miles away.

Lavender likes to be grown in full sun, although in a seriously hot climate, some afternoon shade would be appreciated.

## INGREDIENTS

Filtered water

Ice-cube tray

Edible or safe-to-eat flowers (see right)

Scissors

# Floral Ice Cubes

**These pretty ice cubes get the most amazing reaction every time I produce them. People assume I've been doing elaborate things for hours with tweezers and tiny petals and can't believe how simple they are to make when I explain.**

Use edible or safe-to-eat flowers, such as violets, geraniums, jasmine, pansies (*Viola*), marigold (*Calendula officinalis*), cornflowers (*Centaurea cyanus*), and carnations (*Dianthus*). The ice cubes don't really add anything to your drink tastewise, but because they are so beautiful, they make whatever you're drinking seem like a celebration—perfect for a summery outside lunch party.

1 Bring some filtered water to the boil and let it cool (boiling the water stops bubbles forming and keeps the ice clear, not cloudy).

2 Pour the cooled water into the ice-cube tray, filling a third of each square, and then put in the freezer until frozen.

3 Snip the flower stems to size.

4 Remove the tray from the freezer and lay the petals on top of the ice cubes. Cover with water to the top and return to the freezer until the cubes are frozen through.

NB Resist the temptation to pour all the water into the ice-cube tray together with the petals, as I did the first time I made them. I ended up with petals on the top instead of sitting prettily in the middle...

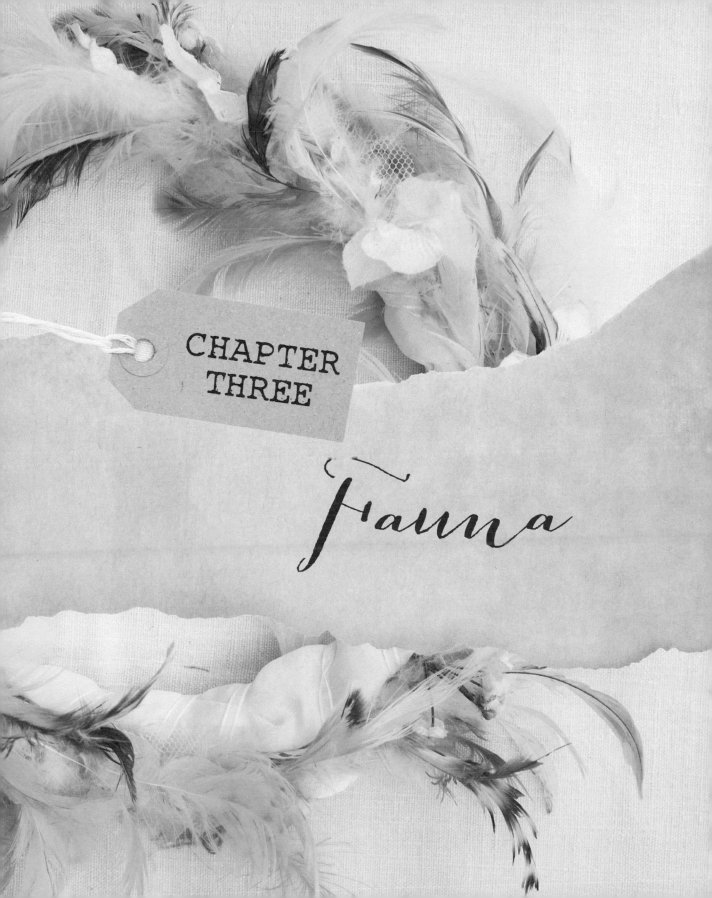

CHAPTER
THREE

Fauna

There's something incredibly beautiful about quails' eggs—their wafer-thin speckled shells look hand-painted and have the palest blue linings. It seems such a waste that they're always thrown away once the eggs have been eaten, and I love that this creation uses the shells whole.

# Quails' Eggs Baubles

Although eggs are usually associated with Easter, I think these make a great alternative to baubles hanging from the Christmas tree. Here, I've hung the eggs from branches of pussy willow (*Salix discolor*) and eucalyptus. Some I painted with gold-leaf paint to make them more festive, but you can paint them any color you like to suit your theme.

I used eggs that had already been blown out. At first, I felt a little guilty about not doing this myself, but that was until I realized that it's actually more expensive to buy intact eggs, and ten times more work. So unless you're mad about quails' egg omelets, I'd suggest doing as I did and hunt down eggs that have already been blown out. If you do decide to do it yourself, it's not particularly difficult, just slightly fiddly, and you need to be as gentle as you can to avoid any crushing. There are bound to be some casualties, so it's better to buy more eggs than you actually need.

1 Paint the eggs with gold-leaf paint, if desired, and let dry.

2 Cut a length of thread at least 20in (50cm) long, thread the needle, and tie the ends together in a little knot. Trim the ends.

3 Carefully poke the needle through the hole in the bottom of the shell (the less pointy end) and pull the thread through the egg and out of the existing hole at the top.

4 Cut the needle away from the thread and tie the ends together at the top of the egg. Trim the ends so the knot is as discreet as possible.

5 Slot feathers into the holes at the top of the eggs, arranging them like a bouquet around the string. When hanging, the eggs will spin around, so they will need to look good from all angles.

## INGREDIENTS

Blown-out quails' eggs

Gold-leaf paint (optional)

Small paintbrush (optional)

Scissors

Long, fine needle and thread, ideally the same color as the foliage

Small, attractive feathers, such as guinea fowl

ADDING GLYCERIN

Add a few drops of glycerin to the
water to stop the eucalyptus from
drying up. I'm not sure how or
why this works exactly, but I do
know that it stops the leaves
from turning a dreary brown and
becoming brittle. Months later they
will still be beautifully green and
pliable.

**One of my favorite discoveries of country life is the singing birds. We started feeding them last spring, and since then their chirping has gone to another level, with a full-on summertime dawn chorus that starts to tune up at three in the morning.**

# Festive Robin

## INGREDIENTS

Green florists' tape

Scissors

Napkin ring

Feather bird with wire feet

Glue gun/super glue (optional)

Natural-colored raffia

Larch (*Larix*) twig with mini cones

Feathers (optional)

Obviously the birds I'm using here can't sing or dance, but they are so lifelike, they could easily be mistaken for the real thing. I hate the idea of birds in cages, so these are the closest I can get to re-creating the great outdoors.

Their wire feet can be twisted to grasp the napkin ring, which is covered in green florists' tape. If you've never used this tape before, let me tell you — it's magic. It's tacky, rather than sticky, which makes wrapping the rings as easy as pie, and they secure the bird really well to the ring.

I am mad about larch branches laden with mini fir cones. I find them on my walks through the woods and always seem to discover a couple lurking in the pockets of whichever coat I put on. If you can't find any twigs with tiny cones, think about using twigs with a small feather instead for the robin's perch.

1 Cut a long length of florists' tape and wrap it around and around the napkin ring, making sure there are no gaps.

2 Secure the bird to the ring with its wire feet. If there is no wire, use a glue gun or superglue instead.

3 Wrap some raffia under and around the bird's feet to secure them further.

4 Slot the larch twig into the raffia, to form a perch. If it feels a bit wobbly, wrap some raffia around it.

5 If you have any feathers to hand, they would look divine slotted into the raffia, almost re-creating a nest.

Every feather I find feels like treasure. I have hundreds of them, but still get excited when I find a new one lying on the ground or poking through the grass. We have them dotted around on surfaces all over the house, propped up in flowerpots and sticking out of glass bottles and pitchers.

# Feathery Treasures

Our friends Jo and Alex collect rare-breed pheasants and when I told them about this book, they turned up on the doorstep with the most enormous box of incredible exotic feathers. It was like Christmas. Spots, stripes, and zigzags, and ridiculously magical colors   it was hard to believe they were real and hadn't been decorated by an artist.

I played around with the feathers for weeks, making headpieces, fans, and mobiles, but decided that keeping things simple was the best way to show them off. I chose to display them *en masse* in narrow-necked, vintage glass bottles, arranged in a big wooden crate. They've been hanging out in our sitting room ever since and get such amazing reactions from visitors that I don't think I'll be moving them any time soon.

A beautiful feather can be a wonderful keepsake. The next time you throw a party or a dinner, try using feathers as the name card holders. Tie the name card to the end of each feather with fine thread.

# Feather Mobile

**I used feathers that I found myself for this mobile. They mostly came from magpies, pigeons, and crows, with an occasional goose feather thrown in for good luck. I jazzed them up a bit by gilding their tips with gold-leaf paint.**

For more impact, as well as gilding the tips, try sprinkling them with fine glitter after painting them. Get creative with the shapes and angles you make with the help of washi tape. Stick small bits of tape onto the feather in the shape you want, then paint between the lines. Don't be impatient and peel the tape off before the paint is dry, otherwise it will run and your straight lines will be no more.

## WORTH ITS WEIGHT IN GOLD

It really is worth investing in gold-leaf paint. Gold spray-paint, which I used initially for this project, just doesn't give the same brilliant, shiny effect.

4

6

## INGREDIENTS

2 lichen-covered sticks, curved so that their ends can be tied together

Natural-colored raffia

Scissors

Gold-leaf paint

Small, flat-edged paintbrush

Selection of feathers

Masking tape (optional)

Cotton thread or string

1 Join the two sticks together at both ends by tying raffia around them. Trim the raffia so there are no long, dangly bits.

2 Shake the pot of gold-leaf paint, then dab gold-leaf paint onto the raffia using the paintbrush.

3 Line up the feathers in the sequence in which you are going to hang them, then choose which ones you want to paint gold at the tips.

4 Simply dip as much of each feather into the paint as you want covered. Let dry, trying not to let the painted area come into contact with anything (I lay them on top of a glass). If you wish to paint stripes or a particular shape on a feather, use masking tape to mark out the area to be painted, then peel it off when you are sure the paint is dry.

5 Let the feathers dry completely (this will take a few hours) before hanging them, otherwise the paint will run. While you are waiting, cut as many lengths of cotton thread as you need (one for each feather).

6 Tie a piece of thread to the quill end of each feather, then tie the other end to a stick. Repeat until all the feathers are in place. Cotton thread blows easily in the wind, so I find it better to attach the feathers to the sticks while the mobile is hanging in place, to avoid any tangles.

**Although I bought these antlers, I would love to discover some for myself while stomping through the Scottish Highlands (deer shed their antlers and grow a new pair every year).**

# Painted Antlers

Antlers are incredibly beautiful to have hanging in their natural state. However, as I wanted to add some color to our sitting room, I decided to cover them with paints left over from decorating the house. They were various shades of blue, so I added in some of my beloved gold-leaf paint to liven things up a bit.

The antlers are covered in tiny blips and ridges, which can make it quite hard to paint straight lines but, with the help of washi tape, it's totally achievable. I specifically chose washi over sticky tape because it's much easier to peel off at the end—sticky tape would take any overlapping paint with it, leaving annoying chips.

1 Lay out the newspaper or protective sheet.

2 Wrap some washi tape around the antlers, according to how wide you want the blocks of color to be. Smooth the tape as you go.

3 Paint the antlers one color at a time (this means less brush cleaning!).

4 When you've finished painting the antlers, let them dry before peeling off the tape to reveal unpainted strips of natural color.

### INGREDIENTS

Newspaper or protective sheet

Washi tape

Pair of antlers

Gold-leaf paint

Decorating paint, in colors of your choice

Small paintbrush, for the gold-leaf paint

Bigger paintbrush, for the decorating paint

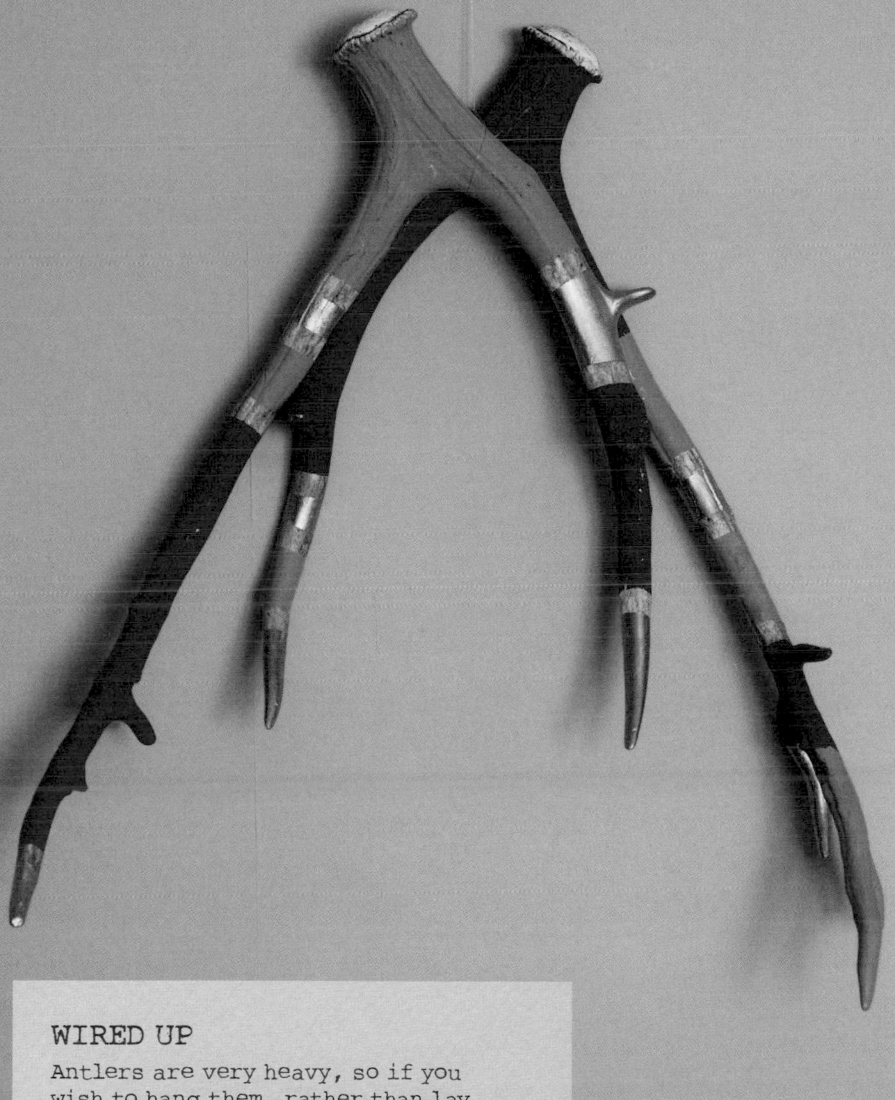

## WIRED UP

Antlers are very heavy, so if you wish to hang them, rather than lay them on a surface, you will need to use something very strong, such as fishing wire. For the antlers shown here, I simply wrapped the wire in and around the antlers until they felt secure and then hung them from a nail.

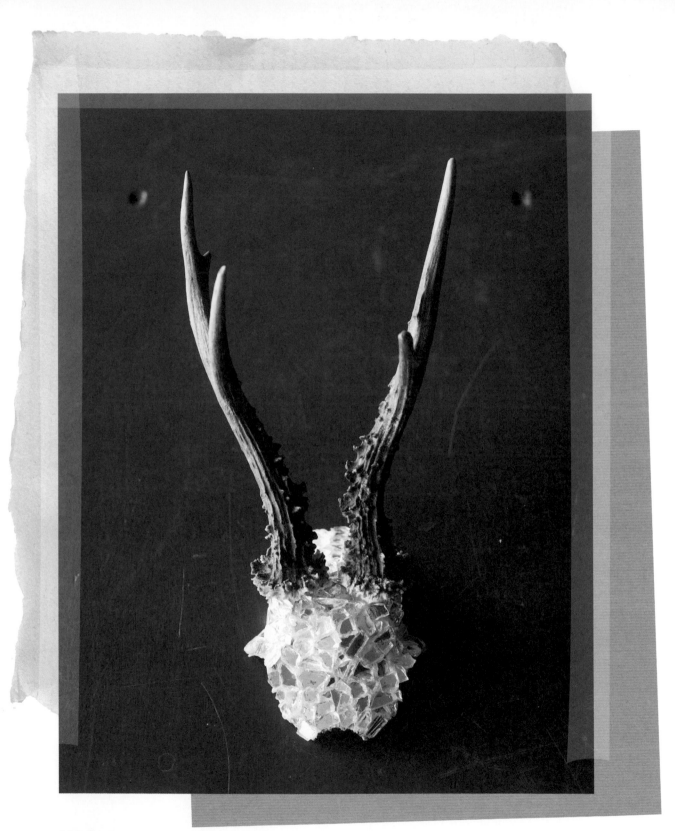

# Glittering Skull

**One of my friends who loves hunting gave me some roe deer skulls. I moved them all around the house for weeks but couldn't decide where to put them.**

I experimented with them in the hall for hanging keys on, in the bathroom as a jewelry holder, or simply mounted on the wall as they were. In the end, I went off-piste when I stumbled upon some mirrored glass mosaics in my office.

These skulls are one of my favorite projects in the book, and they get more admiring comments than anything else I've made.

## INGREDIENTS

Newspaper or protective sheet

Paintbrush

Clear drying glue

Roe deer skull

Mirrored glass mosaics

Pliers or tweezers

Flat-backed wedge of wood, to fit inside the skull and provide a flat surface for mounting

Adhesive plate-hanging disk

Very strong white glue

1 Lay down the newspaper or protective sheet.

2 Paint about one quarter of the skull with a layer of glue.

2

3 Before the glue dries, cover it with the mirrored glass mosaics, using the pliers to pick them up and position them. Keep the mosaics as close together as possible.

4 Repeat until the whole skull is covered, but leave the antlers in their natural state. Let dry for 24 hours.

5 Stick the plate-hanging disk to the flat-backed wedge of wood. If the disk is too big, stick it on and trim to size.

6 Glue the other side of the wood to the inside of the skull, to create a flat surface for mounting.

7 Let the glue dry, and you are ready to hang.

I always feel a bit cruel picking up a bird's nest. We found a few in our garden this year and left them where they were for months, until we were sure that no one was coming back to inhabit them.

# Easter Nests

However, a nest is used only to hold the eggs and protect the young. Most nests are abandoned once the babies are old enough to leave. If you don't like the idea of bringing a real nest inside, it's easy to make your own from moss and twigs and maybe a little fine straw. I love using a mix of genuine (abandoned) nests and homemade ones on the table at Easter. I display them under glass domes, filling them with mini chocolate eggs and hollowed-out quails' eggs, and even a decorative feather bird. Here, I've also added a pretty glass with a bunch of lily-of-the-valley.

## INGREDIENTS

Large shallow dish

Moss, twigs, fine straw

Abandoned nest

Mini chocolate eggs

Hollowed-out quails' eggs

Glass dome

Glass jar

Lily-of-the-valley (Convallaria majalis)

CHAPTER
FOUR

*Beach*

Sea urchins are spiny, spiky creatures that live in oceans all over the world. The pink sputniks used here have been cleaned and had their spikes removed, leaving behind the most heavenly, almost architectural specimens. I am totally crazy about them, and have been using them decoratively since I was about ten years old—their allure still hasn't faded.

# Sea Urchin Table

INGREDIENTS
For a three-tiered candlestick:

3 sputnik sea urchins

Small paintbrush

Superglue

Candle

Here the sea urchins are the star feature of my table setting, becoming candlesticks of various heights as well as salt and pepper holders. I've dressed the rest of the table accordingly, with gentle pinks and whites to keep the theme soft and pretty.

The single-tier candlesticks will look ravishing dotted around the bathtub, too. Also consider using a sea urchin as a vase for air plants. Air plants are epiphytic, which means that they live by absorbing water and nutrients through their leaves, rather than from the soil. You can see what I'm talking about if you have a look at my chambered Nautilus project (see page 128).

If your candles are too short, before gluing take a tiny bit of cardboard and wiggle it gently into the middle urchin, then straighten it out. This will make a raised base for the candle to sit on.

1 Decide which urchins you want to stick on top of each other, starting with the biggest one at the bottom and finishing with the smallest on top. There's often very little difference in their size, but aesthetically this does make a difference.

2 Once you have them in the right order, paint a ring of glue around the top hole of the bottom sea urchin. Glue it to the next urchin.

3 Repeat, so you have three urchins sitting on top of each other. Put a candle inside.

Sea urchins are incredibly fragile.
Keeping them out of the Cubs' hands
is a job in itself as they seem to
think they are felt-tip-pen holders!

# Driftwood Sailboats

**There's something about finding driftwood that excites my imagination. Being a romantic, I get carried away plotting its history, although I know it's probably been washed ashore from a tree rather than an ancient shipwreck. But thinking this way does make beachcombing a real adventure.**

The joy of driftwood is that it's usually well weathered after being churned around at sea, so creating things with it is less of a challenge than you might imagine—nails sink in easily and glue sticks to it well. I've made simple sailboats here, their design dictated by the shape and size of the driftwood. A sail made from a scrap of fabric is an optional extra.

## INGREDIENTS

Pieces of driftwood

Glue gun or superglue

Drill

Fabric for the sail

1 Depending on the size and shape of your driftwood, glue different pieces together to make the hull of the boat. Let it dry.

2 Drill a hole in the hull, to fit the end of the "mast."

3 Put some glue in the hole and insert the mast. Let it dry.

4 Glue a small piece of driftwood to the base of the mast, to make the boom. Let it dry.

5 If you wish to make a sail, glue a scrap of fabric to the mast.

If you're miles away from a beach and can't lay your hands on any driftwood, this may take the romance out of it all, but you can buy huge boxes of it online.

As well as these boats, there are so many other wonderful things you can create with driftwood. Picture frames and heart- and star-shaped garlands are incredibly simple, or you could turn larger pieces into shelves or even build them up to make candlesticks or lamp bases.

# Sea Fan
## Au Naturel

**I think I love sea fans so much purely because I associate them with beach living—my dream white clapboard beach house would be full of them.**

Sea fans come from the tropics and subtropics, which means that for me, living in the UK, they are not that easy to find. Still, I have a couple of them, which I display as they are, *au naturel*, and move them around the house depending on my mood. When I finally get my hands on some more, they will be popped into box frames and hung on my bathroom walls.

Because they are quite fragile, I tend to rest them on something up high, where they won't be knocked over. Here, I've used an antique cotton reel as a display pedestal, which gives added protection as well as prominence, so that the sea fan is the star of the ocean-inspired display.

### INGREDIENTS
Sea fan

Antique thread spool (cotton reel)

Assorted shells, sea urchins, and pieces of coral (optional)

Sea fans may look like plants with their colorful, spiky branches but they're actually animals, just like other corals.

Arrange the sea fans with any other shells and beach treasures you have to create an evolving nautical vignette.

# Orchid Shell

**In a dream world, I would live by the ocean. I love everything about it—the salty air, the crashing waves, even the screeching seagulls. Top, top, top of my reasons, though, would be the never-ending beachcombing opportunities.**

So much of my childhood was spent hunting for shells with my family in Cornwall and on the island of Tresco in the Isles of Scilly. My father and I would spend hours competitively hunting for cowrie shells. The winner would get first pick of the ice creams in the freezer. I've converted Chaz and our children, the Cubs, to my game, although the smaller one has yet to understand that shells aren't for eating.

I admit that I didn't actually find these clamshells myself. Chaz and I were on our first Cub-free vacation in Mauritius and being driven mad by a group of hawkers on the beach. Most of what they had for sale was hideous neon, graffiti-strewn sarongs and mesh vests that gave us electric shocks just looking at them. But they also had a few clamshells, so on day three we gave in and agreed to buy them, provided they would leave us alone for the rest of the vacation. (Naturally, they didn't and were back again, optimistically, the next morning.)

However, I have my shells and love them as souvenirs of our heavenly vacation. Plus, they make original containers, especially when used like this as planters for small orchids. Their shallow shape is perfect, and I find the exotic combination of shell and orchid rather ravishing in my bathroom.

Orchids and I hadn't been the most compatible of companions, so to improve our relationship I asked the experts how to keep them happy. This is what I learned:

• They like natural light, as long as it's north facing and not directly on them.

• They like soft water. If you have hard water, boil it, let it cool, and then give them a drink.

• Overwatering is the most common way to kill an orchid—an eggcup of water once a week is enough.

• Never water the roots when they are green, only when they are a silvery color.

• They loathe drafts, so move them around the house until you find somewhere they like. You will quickly learn if they're not happy.

• Give them orchid feed once a week, following the manufacturer's instructions.

## INGREDIENTS

Large clam shell

Small orchid

Ice cube

1 Gently wiggle the orchid out of its pot, and shake off as much bark compost as you can so that the orchid will fit into the shell.

2 Settle the orchid into the shell, making sure that all the roots are covered in the bark compost (this is what feeds them and keeps them alive).

3 Place an ice cube on top of the bark compost. Enjoy.

My favorite orchid tip is from my wonderful florist friend Charlotte Puxley. Water the plant by putting an ice cube on the bark compost once a week and let the water drip down onto the roots.

# Personalized Pebbles

**The Cubs and I spend a lot of time playing with pebbles, lobbing them into puddles and flower-beds. Unfortunately, throwing pebbles at each other is also one of their current favorite games...**

They know how much I love pebbles and have recently started bringing me their versions of "pretty ones." Their ideas and mine do not always tally, so we have quite a few plain, undistinguished specimens dotted along the windowsills. However, now that they enjoy hunting with me, I have more time to search for proper beauties. I'm very particular and only bring home those I consider perfect. They need to be smooth, buffed by the sea, and, in my dream world, have white lines running through them.

Some people just don't understand this passion and why on earth I would want to clutter up my home with rocks. But I see them as beautiful, calming souvenirs that remind me of vacations. If you want an actual "use" for them, heavy pebbles make good doorstops, while the smaller, perfectly formed ones make original name places on a party table, as described below.

## INGREDIENTS

Pebbles

Gold-leaf paint and paintbrush (optional)

Rub-on transfers, according to the names of your guests

Coin

1 If you wish, paint some of the pebbles with gold-leaf paint and let dry.

2 Take each pebble and, using a coin, rub on transfer letters, one letter at a time, to spell out each guest's name.

**I don't think I could contain my excitement if I actually found a chambered nautilus on the beach. With their graceful, chocolaty-orange zebra stripes and polished white shell, nautiluses are the *crème de la crème* of the shell world.**

# Potted Nautilus

### INGREDIENTS
Newspaper or protective sheet

Chambered nautilus shell

Potted *Sansevieria*

I've found blogs written by people who seem to have dedicated their whole lives searching for a chambered nautilus. I think I probably need to step up a level and go slightly further afield than Cornwall to find one (Australia, Bali, and Thailand are apparently the likeliest places).

These creatures live in tropical waters and have been around for millions of years—they are actually considered to be living fossils, since they've remained virtually unchanged for all that time. As they grow, they expand their living space, adding more and more internal chambers to create a perfect spiral of mother-of-pearl. The body is situated in the final chamber.

The shells have large hollow openings, which make them the most perfect vessel for plants. I've filled mine with *Sansevieria* houseplants, or, as they are more commonly known, snake plants. I don't think many plants would enjoy living in a shell but these are so undemanding, they can survive with very little light and water. I've had mine like this for several months and they couldn't be happier.

1 Lay down the newspaper or protective sheet, and gently remove the *Sansevieria* from its pot.

2 Look at the shell opening to work out how much of the potting compost you need to remove from around the plant to make it fit. Remove as much as you need to.

3 Slot the plant into the shell as deeply and securely as you can. Push in some of the leftover potting compost to fill any gaps.

4 Give the plant a little water, and you're ready to go. Every few days, check to make sure that the potting compost hasn't completely dried out. Water if necessary.

# Gemstone Napkin Rings

**Sadly, I wasn't given the option of studying geology at school. Not that I minded at the time, but now I would love nothing more than to be able to identify all the exquisite gemstones and minerals I keep coming across.**

There are so many to discover, and each one seems more beautiful and mesmerizing than the last. The fact that they also have healing properties makes them even more alluring. I always carry my rose quartz heart in my handbag, which is said to "open the heart to give and receive love."

I have gemstones and minerals dotted all around the house, on tables and windowsills. However, they can sometimes get overlooked or become hidden, so here I attached some amazing agate slices to napkin rings, in order to secure their place in the limelight.

They were very easy to work with—the hardest part was balancing the slices onto the glass napkin rings. Don't worry If you can't get them to balance. Once you slot a napkin through the ring, they will stop wobbling. The main thing you need is very strong glue. And time. Once you've glued the stones into place on the napkin rings, be patient and let them dry for 24 hours.

For a restful night's sleep, place an amethyst crystal under your pillow. It's said to relax and calm the body.

These napkin rings (see below) are slightly less obvious than the agate, but I think they are more sophisticated in an understated kind of way. I made them in the same way as I did the agates, although I painted the napkin rings gold first. The crystals here are much heavier, which makes gluing them slightly harder. If you can find napkin rings with a flat surface, this will make life much easier. I also find that using a gun glue is more effective here than a runny superglue. Leave the napkin rings to dry for as long as you can before using them.

## INGREDIENTS

Newspaper or protective sheet

Superglue/hot glue gun

Glass napkin rings

Slices of agate or other types of quartz or mineral

1 Lay down the newspaper or protective sheet.

2 Put a blob of glue onto each napkin ring and stick down an agate slice.

3 Position the napkin ring so that the agate is face down on your work surface. Let the glue dry for 24 hours.

# Edibles

**Apart from a baked bean can, a cabbage has to be one of the cheapest vases there is. They're easy to get hold of—even my local corner store sells them.**

# Red Cabbage Vase

Allegedly, cabbages have been around since the 1600s, and they are one of the easiest vegetables to grow. I've only shown red cabbages here, but the project works just as well with white and Savoy varieties—I adore the ribbed frilliness of the dark green Savoys. In fact, *en masse*, a mix of different cabbages looks sensational.

What's so clever about cabbages as vases is that the layers of leaves act as natural, ready-made drainage. So whatever you plant in the middle should, in theory, have an equally good chance of living as long as it would in its original pot. I wanted to keep these particular displays quite tonal, so I chose to plant them with cream and dark purple pansies. But, on a crazier day, I would perhaps use hot-pink primulas, and for Christmas, fuchsias and cyclamen.

After a week or so, the cabbages may start to look a bit sad and floppy, especially if the room is quite warm. To perk them up, simply peel back a few layers—the leaves underneath will look as good as new. Ripping the leaves will give a bright white edging and also introduce some texture.

Look after the plants in the same way as you would if they were planted in a regular plant pot. Water them every few days and try not to let them get too hot. I found the pansies were incredibly hardy and even when they looked on the brink of no return, after a good drink they obligingly sprang back to life again—several times, in fact.

WHAT KATIE ATE

Recipes and other BITS & BOBS

KATIE QUINN DAVIES

No. 01

1 Lay out the newspaper or protective sheet and stand the cabbage on top. Using the knife, score a square large enough to accommodate the pansy plant on the top of the cabbage. Position the square as centrally as you can so the plant won't appear lopsided.

2 Cut out the square with the knife, peeling back layer after layer as you dig down—you are essentially making a square hole.

3 Dig down as far as you need, according to the size of the plant. After a while, it will become easier to dig out the filling with the spoon rather than the knife.

4 Remove the pansy from its pot and drop it into the hole. If the plant is too big, gently break off some of the smaller outside roots and shake off any excess potting compost. If the hole is too big, fill in any gaps around the plant with compost.

5 Push the plant in tightly so that it feels snug and secure, and give it a quick drink of water.

## INGREDIENTS

Newspaper or protective sheet

Medium to large red cabbage

Small, very sharp knife

Small spoon

Potted pansy plant

Potting compost

# Painted Squash

**Orange is my least favorite color, yet I'm always bizarrely drawn to squash and pumpkins. I love how they come in so many sculptural shapes and sizes, some cumbersome and knobby, others bulbous and shiny.**

I adore transforming them into creatures for Halloween with the Cubs. Last year, we got slightly carried away and bought far more than we could decorate. They lived on our dining room table for a while until I got sick of the orange and decided to get my paintbrush out.

We had just finished decorating the house, so there were various half-empty paint pots around. The colors were rather low-key neutrals, as you can see from these table-top decorations, but you could paint your squash any palette that suits the setting or occasion. My next batch is going to look completely different: a group of neons followed by a rather gothic matte black arrangement using chalkboard paint.

A pumpkin vase looks wonderful. Cut a circle out of the top with a very sharp knife, but be careful—I've nearly lost many a finger doing this—and then hollow out all the contents inside. You then have a vase ready and waiting. Paint it the same color as your flowers for an original masterpiece.

## INGREDIENTS

Various sizes of squash and pumpkin

Leftover pots of paint

Paintbrush (optional)

If you paint the squash in pale colors, they will need at least two coats. Wait until each coat is dry before applying the next one.

I came across these "peppercorns" on one of my recent flower market missions to Covent Garden, in south London. I had no idea what they were or what I would do with them but just loved how they looked. So, I dropped a few bunches into my basket. Even though they're called peppercorns and look just like the familiar black, red, green, and white ones, they're not even related. They're actually a member of the cashew family.

# Peppercorn Wreath

The "Peruvian peppercorns" (*Schinus molle*) sat on the kitchen windowsill in a vase for months, just hanging out, looking beautiful, until I felt it was time they had a higher profile. After all, they'd traveled all the way from South America and deserved more. My solution was a hanging wreath to suspend above a summery dinner party. Happily, it was incredibly easy to make.

I used entwined vines picked from the garden as the base of the wreath. They are very amenable to work with, stay put, and mean that wires or tape aren't required. The peppercorns are pretty fragile, so do need fairly careful handling. Christmas tree candles and holders provide added sparkle. I suspended my wreath from a big hook that, very handily, hangs above our dining room table.

If you can't get your hands on Peruvian peppercorns, anything with berries would be a lovely substitute—elderberries or even redcurrants would be ravishing. Instead of vines for the wreath base, try anything with pliable, long stems, such as willow (*Salix babylonica*), pussy willow (*Salix discolor*), honeysuckle (*Lonicera periclymenum*), and ivy (*Hedera helix*).

**4** Tie one end of each piece of raffia to the wreath, spacing them evenly. Knot the other ends together securely, for hanging over the hook.

**5** Clip the candleholders to the wreath and insert the candles.

**6** Carefully straighten up the wreath and hang it from a hook. Make sure that the candle flames are nowhere near the lengths of raffia. If necessary, change the position of the candleholders.

## INGREDIENTS

Vines

Bunches of Peruvian peppercorns

Natural-colored raffia

Scissors

Candles and clip-on candleholders

**1** Entwine the vines together. If they don't feel bendy enough and you are worried they may snap, soak them in water for 20 minutes, to make them more flexible.

**2** Lay the wreath flat on your work surface and slot the bunches of Peruvian peppercorns into the gaps between the vines. Tie them in position with short, discreet lengths of raffia.

**3** Cut three equal lengths of raffia, depending on how low you wish the wreath to hang.

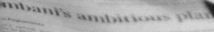

**Strawberries used to be such a treat—an extravagance at summer parties or special picnics in June and July—at least they were when I was little. Call me old-fashioned, but I still think of them as exotic, even though they're to be found year-round in supermarkets, alongside blueberries and kiwis.**

# Strawberry Teapot

I think strawberries are underrated as elegant plants in their own right, especially for the way in which their generous serrated leaves shelter the fruits, which turn from cream to green to pink to scarlet. As the fruits droop down quite low, often far below the leaves, I wanted to pot them into something that would accentuate their habit. Teapots were the answer, particularly as I have something of a penchant for them.

I love using teapots as vases for cut flowers and as containers for bulbs, too, and it's a useful occupation for them if their lids have been broken. Once the strawberries are potted, they take on a rather botanical air and look far too rarified to eat. Treat a teapot as you would any other planter. As it doesn't have any drainage, you will need to create your own with a few stones, grit, or crocks on the base.

Once in position outdoors, the plant will need light and nurturing like any other sun-loving plant. And when its time in the spotlight is over—bear in mind that some varieties do crop twice—it can be repotted in your garden or window box for another year.

What most people don't know (and I certainly didn't) is that strawberries are not berries as such. They're part of the rose family, and the real fruits are the tiny yellow seeds on the outside.

## INGREDIENTS
Stones, grit, or crocks

Teapot

Strawberry plant

Potting compost

1 Add a layer of stones, grit, or crocks to the base of the teapot.

2 Very gently, prize the strawberry plant out of its plastic pot and ease it into the teapot.

3 Add some potting compost to fill in any gaps and stabilize the plant.

# Simply Currants

**I love the vibrant greenness of these unripe blackcurrants, dangling like glass drops below their scented leaves.**

### INGREDIENTS
Blackcurrant stems

Tall, narrow glass vase

I prefer to display blackcurrant stems on their own, without competition from any other flowers. Although it does seem a bit wasteful to pick them before they are ripe, for a special occasion I feel that their beauty warrants it. Be warned, they don't stay perky for especially long—their vase life is hours rather than days.

The unfussy glass vase shows off the currants to perfection and doesn't detract from the arrangement in any way at all. Its height and shape also act as a support for the long stems.

Such simplicity is perfect for a tabletop arrangement at a summer lunch or soirée. Red and white currants would look just as ravishing.

Another option would be to use them garland-style, trailing down a beautifully laid table as the centerpiece Think about adding other late summer fruits and berries into the mix as well. Gooseberries and red- and blackcurrants would look wonderful and make the whole room smell delicious too. Or keep it clean and tonal by simply scattering whole limes and tea lights in and amongst the leaves.

Blackcurrants contain twice the amount of antioxidants as blueberries and are considered one of the best natural sources that you can eat. They're also packed with vitamin C.

**It's the combination of the pink of the radish with the green of their leaves that I love so much. And then I love them all over again when they're cut in half and are bright white with a neon trim.**

# Ravishing Radishes

## INGREDIENTS
Glass jar

Bunch of radishes

White ranunculus

Some of the fancy, non-supermarket versions are even more beautiful, with pink, yellow, and red stripes running through their middles. They quite make me want to take up painting. I feel that they're too pretty to eat, hence this flower arrangement. However, if you do choose to eat them, you're on to a good thing. They are full of antioxidants, great for digestion, very low in fat, and full of folic acid—so a healthy snack if you're pregnant. I'm surprised they haven't made it into the "superfood" hall of fame yet…

When making displays with radishes, you need to be careful about what you pair them with. Their heads are very top-heavy and floppy, so it is up to their companions to support them. Woody-stemmed foliage, ranunculus, and tulips would do the trick, as would ornamental cabbage leaves and broccoli stems, should you wish to pursue the edible theme.

On December 23rd each year in Oaxaca, Mexico, the festival of Noche de Rábanos (The Night of the Radishes) takes place, where craftsmen show off their creations carved entirely from radishes, including Nativity scenes.

# Gilded Pears

**Getting your hands on some of the more unusual ingredients in this book might take a little bit of searching, but this project is so straightforward, you will have no excuse not to try it!**

It's amazing how a little gold paint can transform an everyday fruit into a glistening beauty. I used spray paint here, rather than my favorite gold-leaf paint, which would have been rather extravagant used on this scale. However, if you do happen to have vats of it lying around and can afford to use it, then gild away. It would look incredible.

I mixed the pears with lemons, limes, and beech (*Fagus*) leaves here, as I wanted a fresh feel for a summery dinner. They would also look spectacular in a wintry, Christmas display combined with holly (*Ilex*), ivy (*Hedera helix*), and gold-sprayed dried allium heads.

## INGREDIENTS

Newspaper or protective sheet

Pears of different shapes and sizes

Gold spray paint

1 Lay the pears on sheets of old newspaper and spray them with gold paint. Let them dry completely before applying a second coat. (You may need to spray one side, let it dry, and then turn the fruit over to spray the other side.)

2 Once the paint is completely dry, decorate the length of the middle of the table, mixing the pears with lemons, limes, and beech (*Fagus*) leaves.

**ROYAL HERB-STREWER**

Before proper drainage and medicines became commonplace in England, the job of "royal herb-strewer" (who distributed herbs and flowers throughout the royal apartments to disguise the foul smells of city life) was extremely popular.

# Pots of Herbs

**I adore herbs. There's something so luscious and wholesome about them, and there is nothing better than being able to pick huge, generous bunches of your own rather than removing a few measly sprigs from a supermarket packet. Herbs can completely transform a bland plate of food, and they contain more cancer-fighting antioxidants than most fruit and vegetables.**

The windowsill in our kitchen is bursting with herbs in terra-cotta pots. I used to grow only basil and parsley, but I've since branched out and now grow thyme, sage, cilantro (coriander), dill, sorrel, mint, and rosemary. I'm much more adventurous with my cooking now and adore throwing new flavors into the pot to come up with a new creation.

With the exception of cilantro, these herbs are all surprisingly easy to grow and maintain. Basil is the most forgiving. When you've neglected it, you can bring it back from the dead every time with just a huge glug of water. It's like magic.

## INGREDIENTS

Terra-cotta pots

Herb plants, such as basil, parsley, thyme, sage, cilantro (coriander), dill, sorrel, and rosemary

Potting compost

## INGREDIENTS

Small red chilies

Yellow azaleas

*Alchemilla mollis*

Blue cornflowers
(*Centaurea cyanus*)

Branches of copper
beech (*Fagus sylvatica
atropunicea*)

Sweet Williams
(*Dianthus barbatus*)

Valerian

Aquilegia

Sweet rocket (*Hesperis
matronalis*)

Lupins

Carnations (*Dianthus*)

Campanula

*Tellima grandiflora*

Physocarpus

Long wooden barbecue
skewers

**As far as eating goes, I am not a fan of chilies. I cannot handle spice of any sort; even black pepper is a bit feisty for me. Why anyone would knowingly choose to chili-fy his or her food, I cannot understand.**

# Dazzling with Chilies

My husband Chaz, who loves the kick of chilies and is a brilliant chef, often tests my spice tolerance by secretly adding tiny bits to my food. No one seems to understand that I like my relationship with chilies to be strictly floral.

I can't actually decide if I love or hate this arrangement! There's something quite "bad taste" about it—the in-your-face brightness, the clashing colors, and the general "full-on-ness"—but then I think it's gone full circle. It's so bad, it's good.

I had small red chilies as my starting point, and since there's nothing shy or modest about a chili, the arrangement needed a matching dose of something else to match their exuberance… i.e., the bright, clashing colors of the plants listed on the left. Had it been late summer, I would probably have added fuchsias and orange and purple dahlias to the mix.

To work the chilies into the display, I used wooden barbecue skewers. Simply pierce the chilies with the skewers at whatever angle you want them and then add them in among the flowers for maximum impact.

# Tea Light Artichokes

**If I had to choose one food to sum up the time Chaz and I spent living in France, it would be an artichoke. They hadn't come into my life before we moved there, and then quite suddenly there really was no escaping them.**

An artichoke became our almost daily lunch staple, and now we're living back in England, I miss them like mad. I get ridiculously excited seeing them piled up on a market stall or in a supermarket at the start of the season.

Here, I've displayed them very simply, as tea light holders, but as there's something rather decadent about them, they do suit an opulent, riotous, fit-for-a-prince table setting. They look wonderful incorporated into flower arrangements (technically speaking, the artichoke is a flower bud that has not yet bloomed). You could also add more drama with generous terra-cotta pots of rosemary and sage running down the middle of the table, and sometimes I like to keep the green theme going and mix in Granny Smith apples as additional tea-light holders, too.

If it seems too extravagant to use artichokes for decoration, use cardoons instead, which are ornamental herbaceous artichokes.

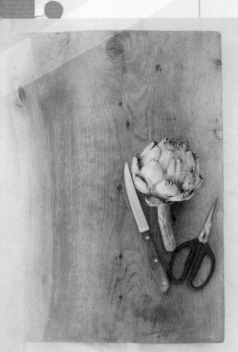

1

3

1 Remove the stalk of the artichoke with the sharp knife or garden clippers, so that the base is flat and stable.

2 Using the knife, slice off the top of the head— about ½in (1cm) across.

3 Open up the leaves from the outside in—this just makes it easier to remove the choke.

4 Cut out the choke in the middle using a pair of scissors. You need to end up with a hole that's just a bit bigger than the tea light.

5 Pop in the tea light, or a pillar candle if you'd prefer more height.

4

## INGREDIENTS

Artichoke

Sharp knife

Garden clippers (secateurs)

Scissors

Tea light or pillar candle

**Being fairly heavy due to their beautiful seeds, pomegranates are not the easiest of fruits to work with. However, I do feel that they are totally worth the wrestle and can transform something quite ordinary into a real showstopper.**

# Pomegranate Showstoppers

Using pomegranates whole has the advantage that their juices won't spill everywhere and stain everything they come into contact with. This arrangement needed to be quite large in scale so that the pomegranates didn't appear too big and out of place. I used mostly branches and foliage from the garden, with a couple of roses and some *Alchemilla mollis* added in to soften it all up.

Incorporating the pomegranates into the display was a bit of a challenge. At first, I experimented with wire, wrapping it around the pomegranates, but they were just too heavy—after an hour or so, I'd find the wire had become detached and they were rolling around on the floor. In the end, I discovered that the best way to hold them in place was to use wooden barbecue skewers.

## INGREDIENTS

Stems of variegated *Cornus*

Stems of dark *Cotinus*, with flowers

Stems of black elderflower (*Sambucus nigra*)

Large pitcher

4 pomegranates

Long wooden skewers

Spray of cream roses

*Alchemilla mollis*

1 Add the *Cornus*, *Cotinus*, and elderflower leaves and flowers to the pitcher, to create the base structure. Move them around until you get the shape you want.

2 Skewer the pomegranates, making sure they are anchored quite firmly, and add them to the pitcher.

3 Fill in any gaps in the display with the smaller, softer flowers of the roses and *Alchemilla mollis*.

## EXTENDING THE THEME

If you plan to use this creation as part of a table setting, think about taking a few more pomegranates and cutting them in half to trail up and down the middle of the table. For a dedicated pomegranate theme, use whole ones as individual name place holders, slotting a little piece of card into the top of the fruit. They look wonderful.

# Sculptural Tomatoes

**I find that adding fruit or vegetables to flower arrangements makes them much more interesting. They bring an added depth, almost, dare I say, a sculptural dimension.**

Tomatoes are one of the easiest fruits to work with and, as they come in so many shapes, sizes, and colors, the designs you can create are endless. Given a choice, I'd always choose unripe tomatoes for their wonderful greenness—but obviously that's not always possible.

I used an actual tomato plant here and potted it into one of my favorite ceramic bowls, which I rested on another upturned bowl to give it extra height. There was no drainage, so I made my own using small pebbles. Once that was in place, I popped the trailing nasturtium (*Tropaeolum*) plants into the mix. I'm not mad about the orange of the nasturtiums, but mingling clashing, bright colors together somehow works, so I introduced some bright red vine tomatoes. These are quite simply hung or balanced from the bowl, and picked when needed.

1 Put a layer of small pebbles in the bottom of the bowl, followed by potting compost.

2 Plant up the nasturtiums, draping their stems over the sides of the bowl, then add the tomato plant.

3 Drape trusses of vine tomatoes from the bowl and on the surrounding surface.

## INGREDIENTS

Small pebbles

Large ceramic bowl

Potting compost

Tomato plant

3 trailing nasturtium (*Tropaeolum*) plants

Trusses of vine tomatoes

# INSPIRATION & SHOPPING

## MY BLOG
www.willowroseboutique.blogspot.co.uk

## SUPPLIES
**Pollen Flowers**
www.pollen-flowers.com

**Abel & Cole** For the freshest fruit and vegetables delivered to your door. www.abelandcole.co.uk

**Covent Garden Flower Market** www.newcoventgardenmarket.com/flower-guide

**C Best, at Covent Garden Flower Market** The best place for florist's sundries—shells, corals, fake flowers, and props. www.cbest.co.uk

**GB Foliage, at Covent Garden Flower Market** If you live in the city and don't have the luxury of picking your own foliage, this is the place to go. www.newcoventgardenmarket.com/users/g-b-foliage

**Ebay** www.ebay.co.uk, www.ebay.com, www.ebay.fr

**Amazon** www.amazon.co.uk, www.amazon.com

## HEAVENLY PLACES TO SHOP AND INSPIRE
**Fade Interiors** Furniture and home accessories. 17 Oxford Street, Woodstock OX20 1TH. www.fadeinteriors.co.uk

**Bluedog & Sought** Interiors and trinkets. 5 Park Street, Woodstock OX20 1SJ. www.bluedogandsought.co.uk

**Kempton Antiques Fair** Every second Tuesday morning. Go early as it closes around midday. www.sunburyantiques.com

**Ashman's Vintage** Wonderful vintage fashion and homeware in Welshpool, Mid Wales www.ashmansvintage.com

**Jas des Roberts** My favorite Sunday morning flea market in a big dusty field, just outside St Tropez. Go early as it shuts down by 1pm. www.jasdesroberts.com

**Oka** Furniture and home accessories www.okadirect.com

**Taman Antik** Home and garden treasure trove in St Tropez. www.tamanantik.com

**Le Club 55** Beach boutique in the south of France. www.club55.fr

**Worton Organic Garden** Amazing market garden with a fabulous farm shop and cafe. www.wortonorganicgarden.com

**Petersham Nurseries** Wonderful nursery, shop, and cafe. www.petershamnurseries.com

**Pitt Rivers Museum, Oxford** The most intriguing and fascinating museum. www.prm.ox.ac.uk

**Deyrolle** A Parisian shop styled like a cabinet of curiosities. www.deyrolle.com

**Sarah Raven** The gardening guru's website full of tips and advice. www.sarahraven.com

**Cabbages & Roses** Most heavenly clothes, fabrics, and interior treats. www.cabbagesandroses.com

**Old Pill Factory.** 22 little vintage shops under one roof in Witney. www.theoldpillfactory.com

**Daylesford Organic** Eat, shop, and spa in organic bliss. www.daylesford.com

**Odd** Heavenly oddities and home of the wondrous Old Rocker. www.oddlimited.com

**Salvoweb** A great online resource www.salvoweb.com

**Beyond France** Vintage linen, sourced from all over Europe. www.beyondfrance.co.uk

**International antiques and collectors fairs** Comprehensive online listings of fairs. www.iacf.co.uk

**Anthropologie** Home accessories and clothes. www.anthropologie.eu www.anthropologie.com

**Rachel Ashwell** Furniture, furnishings, and fabrics from the queen of Shabby Chic. www.rachelashwellshabbychiccouture.com

**Terrain** House, home, and outdoor living. www.shopterrain.com

**Pimpernel & Partners** Furniture and home accessories. www.pimpernelandpartners.co.uk

**Sibella Court** The website for this amazing Australian stylist. www.thesocietyinc.com.au

**The Old Flight House** Antiques, vintage, and interiors in Oxfordshire. www.theoldflighthouse.co.uk

**Lassco** Architectural antiques, salvage, and curiosities. www.lassco.co.uk

**The Cloth House** Incredible fabrics, new and old. www.clothhouse.com

**Green and Stone** Old-fashioned art materials shop in Chelsea, London. www.greenandstone.com

**American Home and Garden Store** Vintage furniture and furnishings in downtown Ventura. www.ahgventura.com

**Atelier de Campagne** A Californian warehouse bursting with European vintage treasures and antiques. www.atelierdecampagne.webs.com

**Remnants of the Past** An incredible vintage market full of exciting different sellers in California. www.remnantsofthepast.com

**The Huntington** For a guaranteed magical day out, head to Pasadena to the most mesmerizing 120 acres of gardens. www.huntington.org

**Little Flower School Brooklyn** For lessons in creating loose, natural, garden-focused floral designs in NYC. www.littleflowerschoolbrooklyn.com

**Saipua** Most ravishing flowers and hand made soaps in Brooklyn NYC. www.saipua.com

**www.gardenista.com** An online sourcebook for cultivated living.

**www.designsponge.com** Website dedicated to all things home; DIY, shopping, entertaining and treasures.

# INDEX

# Acknowledgments

I would like to say a huge thank-you to:

Chaz. For loving, supporting, and putting up with me through another book. I couldn't do anything without you. Thank you, thank you, thank you for your advice, patience, and magic calming powers.

My baby Cubs, Wolf and Rafferty. For all your help collecting treasures and for putting up with me staring at my laptop for hours on end.

Mama. This book should have your name on the cover. I really really couldn't have done this one without you. Thank you for all your styling, cooking, editing, ideas, arranging, and picking. For being my plant guide, dictionary, thesaurus, and all-round magical guru in one.

Emma, the most wonderful photographer. Thank you for taking such heavenly photographs. For calming me and letting me be indecisive and bossy. You are a dream to work with. Thank you.

Da. For letting me take Mama away from you for days on end.

Ned. For lending me your wonderful props.

Tom. For making me laugh.

Katie. This would absolutely not have been possible without you. Thank you for looking after those Cubs so incredibly. We are so lucky to have you. Thank you.

Sally, Gillian, and Cindy at CICO Books. For taking another risk on me and letting me create this book. For your designing, editing, and endless day-to-day support and encouragement.

Helen. For your unbelievable patience and brilliant editing.

Laura. For your wonderful design and layout skills.

Mel. For all your support, encouragement, and endless prop lending.

Lou. For continually offering up your garden for raiding.

Alex and Jo. For those incredible feathers.

Hunter and Rose. For so generously providing and cleaning the skulls.

Home Barn in Little Marlow, and Bluedog & Sought and Fade in Woodstock. For so generously lending me your most wonderful stock. This book would not look the same without you. Thank you.

The wonderful Pollen florist team. For letting me stand dillydallying for hours in your shop. For your advice, your time, help, and patience.

Jane Thomas. For your identifying skills.

My wonderful Aunt Daffy. For lending me the beautiful alliums.

Anneke and David at Worton Organic Garden. For allowing us to shoot in your heavenly café.

Anna Dewar. For letting us take over your house.

Rosie Bartlett. For lending me your wonderful olive oil drums.

Clare Hulton. For getting me this magical second book deal!